Hit Your Grand Slam

Rounding Life's Bases in a Chase for Greatness

Mark A. Martinez

STREAMLINE
BOOKS

HIT YOUR GRAND SLAM

Rounding Life's Bases in a Chase for Greatness

Copyright © 2023 by Mark Martinez

All rights reserved.

Ornamental break images and Base Study section header images Designed by Freepik.

Cover Design by Will Severns

Streamline Books

www.WriteMyBooks.com

Paperback ISBN: 9-798-3745-4481-7

Hardcover ISBN:

March 1st, 2023

Acknowledgments

Thank you to my amazing wife, Tracy. I love the way you strike the perfect balance of encouragement, belief, and accountability. What a blessing you are to me. I love you dearly.

Thank you to my children, Marquelle, Mimi, Cade, and Nico. Thank you for being my Why, and keep Chasing your Destiny.

Thank you to my Mom, Dad, and Sister. From Onzaga to King Drive you provided me with the perfect launching pad.

Thank you to my third baseman, Bob. You and your family were just what I needed at the time I needed it. And you still are today.

Thank you to Josh, Larry, Fred, and The Locker Room. There is no Grand Slam without the Locker Room. Thanks for loading up the bases for me.

Thank you to Doug and Gary. Can't think of two better guys to get lost in the woods with.

Thank you to The Mules. If only every kid could have the memories we created Around the Way.

Thank you to JT and The International 10. We have a Bond like no other.

Thank you to Matt & Team Streamline. What you guys do is unbelievable. I'm so appreciative of your talents and giftings.

To my Grandmother, Mildred. I feel your love everyday and miss you so much. The memories you created for me and Lisa continue to provide us with such warmth and joy. You are truly The Greatest of All Time!

Contents

Foreword
By Billy Severns

For Mark, many of his stories start with baseball, getting out of the dugout and stepping into the batter's box. It all starts at home plate. Baseball is the only game that begins at home and ends at home. But trust me, it only begins there. There is "encouragement" for every single one of us in the following pages:

To the individual who feels like they are "striking out" at every turn, or in the bottom of the 9th with 2 strikes against them. (baseball just says it best sometimes!)

To the "mom and dad" who have been searching for a balance in managing the myriad of things on their plate.

To the business man or woman who has

been chasing the wrong things at the expense of family or health.

To the youth who feel like they don't measure up and have been lied to about what "greatness" should look like.

And finally to the student, athlete, or individual that is struggling to come to grips with falling short of their dreams.

When I first met Mark, a mutual friend had asked me to go to lunch and hear his thoughts about this book. It was an extremely uplifting meeting. Mark is clearly answering a call in his life. In baseball, we used to say, "one day it'll click". I have seen this hundreds of times in my work where all of a sudden somebody says, "I see it. I think I'm pretty good at this and I think it is fun". It is a great thing to see. Everyone is born to do something special and God has a plan for them. I believe that with all my heart and Mark does too.

At that lunch, we almost began shouting with excitement about this book. And it was the first time we had ever met!! In all of my years of playing collegiate baseball and toiling for 6 years in the minor leagues, I had never hit a "Grand Slam" that Mark talks about. I was a "get on base" guy with a pretty good batting average and good speed around the bases, but I was usually the runner on base when the "big hitter" came through with the longball. Hey, we all have our roles right?

I remember the joy of rounding the bases just ahead of the slugger. It was no less thrilling.

In this day of Aaron Judge and the emphasis on "big flies," we certainly revere the clout; but if you watch the fans screaming with joy and teammates flying out of the dugout, (to participate in the victory "dog pile" at home plate), you realize that baseball and life have a lot in common.

It is meant to be played, lived, appreciated, and celebrated with those we love.

Mark is calling all of us to trust God and dream bigger dreams. Ephesians 3:20 is a great verse. "Now to Him who is able to do immeasurably more than all we may ask or imagine, according to His power that is at work within us." The world needs more dreamers. Even with all of the stressful times, there is always someone who is dreaming of a better world. You see it every day. Mark wants to help you get there. Enjoy his exhortation to you. He is encouraging you to apply God's work and power to your life. Just like the promise in Ephesians, <u>God can outdream you, outthink you, has a bigger plan than you have, and is challenging you to trust Him.</u> Take Him up on His offer!! Keep moving, be patient, and have faith.

So like Mark says, "grab a bat, step up to the plate, take your place in the batter's box and swing the bat." You can't hit it if you don't swing!

Good luck, it's Game Day!!

Pre-game: The Locker Room

There are few moments in sports as breathtaking or as memorable as a grand slam in baseball. They can turn a routine at-bat into a world-historical event, a career-defining act, or a miracle of mythological proportions. Grand slams are so rare that witnessing one live feels almost sacred, and yet so ubiquitous that every baseball-loving 8-year-old has imagined stepping up to the plate down three runs in the bottom of the ninth with the bases loaded. And unlike hitting for the cycle, batting .400, or knocking in 100 RBIs in a season, a grand slam can happen in a single at-bat, and it doesn't take an all-star to hit one.

In fact, Derek Jeter, arguably the most recognizable face in baseball over the last thirty years, only hit one grand slam in his entire career. Ozzie Smith, one of the greatest St. Louis Cardinals to ever wear the red bird, never hit one at all. And it took Slammin' Sammy Sosa, a hitter known for mashing home runs at the same pace most players hit singles, almost 250 home runs before he hit his first grand slam.

Even more astonishing is that the classic childhood baseball scenario, a grand slam with the team down three, bases loaded, and two outs in the bottom of the ninth inning, has only happened 32 times *in the entire history of recorded Major League Baseball.* And while some of them were hit by the game's biggest players (Babe Ruth being the first on record to do so in 1925), what is so amazing about a game-winning grand slam is that among the great game-defining moments, it is incredibly democratic. You don't need to be the best hitter in the world, you don't need to compete for the batting title, and you don't need to throw a perfect game or win a Gold Glove for a season of incredible defense. All you need to do is step into the batter's box at the right moment and take advantage of a single opportunity. And if you do that, you can find your name on the same list as Babe Ruth and Roberto Clemente. I'm looking at you, David Bote.

Recently, it has dawned on me that my chances of playing Major League Baseball have seriously diminished. And if you're anything like me, you may have kissed goodbye your dreams of playing in the majors too. Or maybe you've never put on a baseball glove, can't throw a paper airplane, and wouldn't dream of hitting a ball with a stick even ten feet, let alone over a 300-foot fence. Maybe you've never heard of Derek Jeter, or God forbid, even Babe Ruth. Maybe before you read the last few paragraphs, you thought a grand slam was just an iconic menu option at your favorite restaurant. That's okay.

I'm here to tell you that you can still hit one.

Okay, let me clarify. Statistically speaking, it is highly unlikely that you are going to hit a grand slam in a Major League Baseball game.

That is unfortunately reserved for .00001% of humans who have ever lived. But what if I told you that you could hit a grand slam that matters much more than four runs on a scoreboard of a single baseball game? What if there was a grand slam that would mean more for your life than even a game-winning home run with the bases loaded? What if there was a way that someone with very little hand-eye coordination and no athletic prowess could hit a grand slam that would truly matter, a grand slam that would dramatically impact not only that person's own life but reverberate into the lives of everyone they know?

I'm talking, of course, about the fly-fishing grand slam.

That's a joke. (Not the existence of a fly-fishing grand slam, mind you, which we will discuss in detail later on.) I'm talking about hitting a grand slam *in life*. About stepping up to the plate each day, staring down the pitch that is coming your way, and taking a swing at greatness. I'm talking about living a life that will make an impact and leaving a legacy that will be a blessing. This might not have the glamour of a grand slam in baseball, but trust me, it has all the value and more.

Taking the grand slam as our guide, this book is going to walk you through what it looks like to hit a grand slam in life, and how hitting a grand slam on the baseball diamond can teach you something about greatness in your marriage, in your family life, at work, or wherever else you hope to achieve it. Along the way, you'll get to hear from real people who have chased greatness in their own lives, and hit their own grand slams. After each chapter, you'll find a "Base Study," an example of a person whose own life embodies the principles associated with that base, and who models for you as a reader what greatness could look like for you.

As in baseball, in life, it is not easy. Hitting a grand slam in life requires a lot of hard work. It requires a willingness to step up to the plate after a bad strikeout, or even a whole season of slumping. It takes intentionality and a burning desire for greatness. Like anything truly worth doing, it is difficult. But this book will give you the tools you need to take what is left of your life and knock it out of the park.

There will be a lot to say about approaching the plate, running the bases, and coming home. Those are the most obvious parts of the grand slam: the disciplined at bat, waiting for the right pitch, and the iconic trot around the bases to the sound of organized mayhem. We will come to these in due course. But first, a word about what the fans do not see, what doesn't make the highlight reels, what flies under the radar of a grand slam but which is crucial for any great moment in team sports.

I'm talking about the locker room. You can't hit a grand slam in life or baseball unless you have the right locker room environment. The locker room is at the heart of all team success. Everything in sports ties back to the locker room, and, as we will see, everything in the grand slam life ties back to having a healthy "locker room" as well.

As those who have played team sports know, some of the best (and worst) moments in a career happen in the locker room. It is a kind of mythical place where teams come together, take off their street clothes, put on a common uniform, and mentally, physically, and emotionally prepare, as a team, for the upcoming game.

The locker room is a place to hang out, to kill time before a game, to stretch and receive treatment for injuries, and to game plan. But more than anything, the locker room represents a safe space, a place for vulnerability. It is a place where people get naked, certainly physically, but also emotionally.

The locker room is an especially unique place for men in our society. Modern men are notorious for their difficulty with vulnerability. While isolation is a problem for almost everyone these days, it is men in particular who struggle to make friendships, to share the difficulties and joys of their lives with others, and to find others who will hold them accountable to the promises they've made, and the ways they've pledged to live their lives. The locker room stands nearly alone in our world as a place where all of these things are not only allowed, but actually encouraged.

And, as any good coach knows, the relationships that are built in the locker room don't stay there. They carry over onto the field. Truly great teams don't just want to win for the fans, they want to win for each other. Grand slams are far more meaningful when the people on base are more than just co-workers or teammates.

Life's grand slams happen on the field, not in the locker room. If you never leave the safety of the locker room and step into the batter's box, you'll never hit a grand slam. But it's much easier to live a truly great life, to hit a grand slam, if you are surrounded by team-mates—family, friends, mentors, and others—who support you and truly know you. Contrary to what much of our world thinks, strength and vulnerability are not opposites. Sharing your life with others, mourning their losses, carrying their burdens, and celebrating their victories is not a sign of weakness, but a sign of fortitude, health, and wisdom. This is what happens in the locker room, and it's why a healthy locker room is essential for the grand slam life.

So who is in your locker room? Who do you let see your real self? <u>What are you doing to cultivate a community that can share in the burdens and beauty of life with you</u>? How are you allowing others to keep you accountable, to hold you to high standards, and to call you out when you need it? Do you have a mentor? Are you mentoring others?

Thinking about these questions is the first step to hitting a grand slam in life. You need encouragement in the dugout, you need runners on base, and you want a champagne shower after the game. Focusing on your locker room will make sure all these things are in place and position you to succeed when you finally step into the box with the bases loaded.

Base Study: The Locker Room

Bob (80) | *OLATHE, KS*

Several years ago at our church, folks were encouraged at the start of each January to come up with a focus word for that year. The word chosen was supposed to function as a sort of personal theme for the year. The word I came up with was *intentional*. Shortly after that word came to me in church, there was a listing of the classes that were going to be held. One of them was a class on The Intentional Man, and that's where I got started with the Locker Room.

Pre-game: The Locker Room

The "Locker Room" was a place where men could come in, and talk freely about what was going on in their lives and get input from other guys in the group. Whatever was discussed in the Locker Room stayed in the Locker Room, so men could feel free to open up. Sometimes we would have 12 people, sometimes we would have closer to 30, and guys would come and go as they felt comfortable. I was in the class for probably seven or eight years, and I was one of the older people in class. We shared all sorts of things, whether it was job-related or marriage-related or about other relationships or situations, and got feedback from the group, often from somebody else who had experience. It was all encouraging, and it was a safe place for men to come in and visit.

For me, the focus was on who I was in my relationship with my wife. I realized that there were things I could have done, should have done, and didn't do. I wanted to change that and become a better person and a better husband for her, but I didn't necessarily know how to start. My time in the Locker Room was instrumental in helping me figure that out. And the feedback I got, especially from my wife, was really positive. She saw a change and noticed the positive direction of our relationship. Now we're both so much more pleased in our marriage—it wasn't a bad relationship, but now it's so much better.

A lot of the change came from my new understanding and appreciation of my wife and what she brings to our relationship. There were a lot of things that I was able to talk about in the Locker Room, and it was enlightening for me, teaching me things I did not understand before. Talking with other men about my marriage really opened my eyes. We had profound discussions about our emotions, and I was able to truly open up about my own feelings. The Locker Room gave me the tools to do that, along with a better understanding of how I fit into the relationship between my wife and me. Now the marriage we have is so much richer. It has allowed her to be more open with me in turn, which has strengthened our friendship and our marriage, and that has been a blessing.

And it wasn't just me. There were men that talked about their relationships with their fathers or their mothers and how those relationships would affect their relationship with their spouses. There was a lot of that dialogue, and it set the tone and created a healthy understanding. For me, reflecting on my father's relationship with my mother allowed me to see how I was paralleling part of that in my own marriage. They had a good relationship and were married for over 60 years, but it wasn't perfect. Once I saw that and listened to some of the other guys speak about the relationship between their parents I knew something was missing and I needed to make some changes, because I had the desire to have a stronger relationship with my wife.

There were a lot of times when guys came into the Locker Room and they were hurting, I mean tears and everything. It was often very emotional and heartfelt, very genuine. And I think this allowed for a lot of healing to happen. It was just a safe place to be able to open up and get feedback from other men. Typically, conversation between men (and women too!) can be very surface-level. *How are you doing? How are you feeling? Fine.* Everybody feels fine. But when you get into the Locker Room and you really get to hear what's going on in the lives of others, there's a bonding that takes place. That all came out in the Locker Room.

— Bob Courtney, *Grand Slam: A Better Marriage*

Base Study: The Locker Room

VINCE (64) | *SHAWNEE, KS*

I struggled with various addictions growing up. I grew up in a home with a father who was emotionally and physically abusive at times with some family members. My dad was a functional alcoholic. He worked every day and paid the bills, but we had no real relationship. He was there as a disciplinarian, and it was tough growing up without having a healthy father figure to relate to. And so I think the first big thing that struck me about the Locker Room was that there were a couple of elder statesmen, you might say, that were part of the group. These were guys who were retired, in their seventies, and had raised their families. So they were like father figures or grandfather figures to some of us. The Locker Room was the first consistent place for me to build relationships with other men that were healthy, honest, transparent, and consistent, and to get to know other men well.

The Locker Room was an environment where I could relate to other men in an honest way. For a significant part of my life, I struggled with a cocaine addiction, which cost me dearly. But by the grace of God and the help of other people involved in my life, it didn't ruin my career. And with the help of another men's group that was more addiction focused, that addiction was broken. For more than 22 years I've been clean. God broke that addiction, brought me a wonderful wife with whom I could be honest and share my story, and walk out of that phase into a whole new life.

Pre-game: The Locker Room

The Locker Room is a place of trust where you know, "That's my brother there. He knows my story and we're walking the same road. Even though we may have different things we're walking through, we're still walking in the same direction. We've got each other's backs, we pray for each other, and encourage each other." It's not superficial. It's not just built on hanging out and watching football on Sunday. It is built on knowing each other's stories and sharing each other's struggles; sharing goals, dreams, and hopes for the future. In most places today, it is really difficult to get to know anybody like that.

— Vince Martini, *Grand Slam: Overcome Addiction*

Chapter 1
The Batter's Box

Baseball stadiums, especially those that house Major League teams, are massive structures. The rules of the game mandate that there must be a distance of at least 325 feet from home plate (unless you're the New York Yankees) to the right and left field walls and a whopping 400 feet from home plate to the center field wall. Most ballparks exceed these distances (Comerica Park, the home of the Detroit Tigers, has the furthest current center field wall at 422 feet). It's well known that 90 feet lie in between each base, and 60 feet and 6 inches separate the pitching rubber from home plate. Baseball is a game of inches and feet, a game where a pitch that crosses the plate a finger's breadth too high or low could result in a free pass to first base, or a ball being blasted a football field and a half into the upper deck in left field.

An average baseball park has an area of over 110,000 square feet, yet the heart of the game takes place in the 4 by 6-foot rectangles on either side of home plate. Just as the heart of the unfathomable expanse of the universe lies on our tiny little planet, so the heart of the ballpark sits at home plate, a 17-inch wide rubber slab, coming to a point 17 inches from the center of its back edge. It's the corner of the universe´ from which the ball field expands out infinitely into space, where fair territory knows no limit.

If you can forgive the poetic imagery, the batter's box has a kind of cosmic significance. It is the vantage point from which a baseball player sees the whole of the game. It is the pinnacle of opportunity, the almost-sacred place where, weapon in hand, the batter stands in crowded solitude, the lone representative of his team amid nine others intent on sending him back to the depths from which he came. The batter's box is the home of the greatest moments in the game—earth-shaking cracks of the bat, bunts, bloops, and blasts that bring home game-winning runs, and, of course, grand slams. And yet, it is also the place where the most fundamental (and most common) failure of the game occurs: *the strikeout.* All of the greatest hitting streaks in baseball history have started in the batter's box. Likewise, every strikeout, slump, and sour season happens with a batter standing in a rectangle to the right or left of home plate.

If you want to hit a grand slam, you're going to have to face the terror and triumph of the batter's box and work through those situations that feel like you've just been hit by a pitch.

One of the most beautiful things about baseball is that it is a game of repetition, which means it's a game of opportunities. Where you may only get a few clean looks from the three-point range in a basketball game, or one great chance at scoring in a soccer match, baseball's rules guarantee that, as long as you stay in the game, you're going to step up to the plate around three to four times for a chance to put the ball into play.

The batter's box is a place of triumph and terror, but it is also a place of opportunity.

And so the first thing to say about stepping into the batter's box is that it is not a singular event.

If you spent any time on the internet from 2010 to 2015 (if you didn't, I'm both concerned for and proud of you all at once), you might be familiar with the acronym "YOLO," short for "You Only Live Once." Calling YOLO an acronym is probably underselling it. It might be better described as a mantra or a lifestyle. You'd be just as likely to see it tattooed on someone's shoulder or hear it screamed as someone launches out of an airplane skydiving as you would to see it hashtagged on an Instagram post. In one sense, the animating principle behind YOLO is right in line with the heart of the grand slam life. You only have one life, and you should do what you can to live it as best as you can.

But in another way, YOLO communicates something completely opposed to the grand slam mindset. While you only have one *life*, you *live* every single day. As others have said, the thing you only do once is *die*, but the goal is to *live* every day, to take each day as a new opportunity to embrace your life and make it all that it can be.

This is the grand slam mindset, and it is why the batter's box is so crucial to hitting a grand slam. Stepping into the batter's box is not a one-off occurrence. It's not something you only get one shot at in baseball. In fact, one of the most important stats in baseball is the batting average, which depends for its value on a hitter making many, *many* trips to the batter's box. The baseline batting average in Major League Baseball typically lands somewhere around .250, which means that on average, a batter only gets a hit one time every four trips to the plate. And if you think about how rare grand slams are among hits, you can get a feel for how many times a hitter steps into the batter's box before hitting a grand slam.

So HITTING your grand slam is going to take determination, it's going to take burning desire, and it's going to take stick-to-it-ness.

This can be scary. Stepping into the batter's box is not always an easy thing. Likewise, really trying to change your life, really chasing greatness, takes serious effort, and it can be scary. Failure is painful, and it often leaves scars. If you've struck out before or been hit by a pitch, the batter's box can feel like a real risk, and that's because it is! A 100-mile-per-hour fastball coming your way is no joke.

But the beauty of the batter's box for the grand slam life is that, despite what you've heard from Eminem, you don't only get one shot. You only have one life, true, but you get to live every day. Each new day is another at-bat, another chance to see some pitches, another opportunity for a grand slam.

Every day you have a chance to wake up and commit yourself to excellence in your life. Every day you have a chance to wake up and be a friend. Every day you have a chance to wake up and make sacrifices for your children. Every day you have a chance to wake up and work hard with integrity at your job. And if you strike out, the good news is that you're going to get another at bat.

There is Purpose in your Past!

This is all easy to imagine when things are generally going well, when you're coming off a great season where you hit .315 and just signed a fancy new contract. But when you're slumping, when you don't feel like you could hit water if you fell out of a boat, stepping back into the batter's box gets a lot more difficult. It takes courage. It takes a burning desire for greatness.

So maybe you're reading this and you're in the middle of a slump. Maybe you haven't prioritized your family, and things are falling apart. You don't feel like you can talk to your spouse anymore, and the love and friendship that used to be there seem to have faded. Now it feels like you are just two strangers living in the same house, trying to hold things together for your kids. Or maybe you have spent so much time in the office that your kids don't even expect to see you before they go to bed anymore. They're more familiar with your voice on FaceTime than they are in real life. What started as providing them with a good life has turned into them living their lives without you present. Or maybe you've been phoning it in at work for years because you hate your job, but you can't imagine doing anything else. Your relationship with your boss has soured, and you're full of resentment for your colleagues who have made advances in their careers or moved on from this job while you feel so stuck.

Whatever your slumping situation is, I'm here to tell you that *you can still hit your grand slam in life*. Your failure doesn't have to be forever. The pitcher is on the mound, and the batter's box has been freshly painted. The bases are loaded, and you are due up. Your batting average doesn't matter now. Neither does the fact that you are hitless in your last twenty at-bats. All of that can change on a dime. What matters now is the decision in front of you. Will you step back into the batter's box of your life? Will you take the risk of committing yourself to change? Will you let your past failures define you and consign yourself to broken relationships and missed opportunities? Will you let complacency win? Or will you chase greatness?

Chasing Greatness

What you've decided to do by stepping into the batter's box, either for the first time or the five thousandth, whether in the middle of a streak or a slump, is to chase greatness. And chasing greatness is at the very core of what it means to live the grand slam life. Without the chase for greatness, without burning desire, there is no grand slam.

So what does greatness look like? Well, what kind of grand slam are you shooting for?

Remember when I told you there was a fly-fishing grand slam? Well, that was just the tip of the iceberg's tip.

While the baseball grand slam is undoubtedly the most iconic of all grand slams, the sheer amount of other grand slams is enough to make the words "grand slam" start to sound like nonsensical mouth mush because you've said them so many times.

There are the grand slams you've probably heard about. The Tennis Grand Slam (winning all four major tournaments) or the Golf Grand Slam (ditto). Perhaps you've heard of the NASCAR Grand Slam, in which one person wins all the Cup Series majors in one year. I know my equestrian daughter Mimi has heard of the thoroughbred horse-racing Grand Slam, which is the Triple Crown plus one other major race in the same season. And you already know about the (Caribbean) Fly Fishing Grand Slam, which is when one person catches a bonefish, a tarpon, and a permit all in one day of fishing.

Wow, you might be saying, that's a lot of grand slams. My friend, I have only scratched the surface.

There are also grand slams in sports (to use the term loosely) as diverse as:

- Pro wrestling
- Curling
- Ultra-running
- Darts
- Figure skating
- Rugby
- Roller derby

- Ski-jumping
- Shinty (look it up)
- Filipino Association Basketball
- Ocean Exploring
- Pan-Continental adventuring
- Show business (also known as an EGOT: Emmy, Grammy, Oscar, Tony)

Did I mention roller derby[1]?

And we would be remiss to forget what is perhaps the greatest iteration of the grand slam: two buttermilk pancakes, two beef bacon strips, two sausage links, and two eggs at your local Denny's[2]. I just checked the website; they are in stock.

That's a lot of grand slams. And while many of them have some relationship to the number four, that's basically where the similarity ends.

Except for this one essential characteristic: they are all metrics of greatness for their sport, game, practice, or well-rounded breakfast.

As much as I'd love to spend the next thirty-plus pages describing each of these grand slams in detail, the central point to make is this: *each of these grand slams is different, but all of them are great.* All of them require a burning desire to achieve. But the path to these different kinds of greatness and the skills required to get there are not the same. The skills and practice necessary to hit a grand slam in baseball are significantly different from those necessary to win four Cup Series Nascar races, run 400 miles on foot, or hit repeated triple twenties in darts. There is no single kind of greatness or skill behind all of these incredible feats. In each case, greatness is defined by the goal that one sets out to achieve.

If you're shooting for the curling grand slam, you probably don't need to take acting classes. If you want the WWE grand slam, you'll want to spend your time in bars fighting, not throwing darts. The hand-eye coordination, core strength, and bat speed necessary to hit a grand slam in baseball won't be very helpful when you're trying to land a triple axel in figure skating. You get the point.

The same is true as you consider what the chase for greatness looks like in your own life.

I wish I could tell you that there is a simple formula for living a truly great life or for hitting your grand slam, and that you just need to follow five easy steps to achieve true greatness. But the reality is that life is not that simple, and greatness is not that straight-forward.

Greatness is contextual. It depends on your particular situation and the goals that you set for your life. It depends on what kind of grand slam you want to hit. Hitting a grand slam in your friendships will require different things from you than hitting a grand slam in your job. Hitting a grand slam with your employees will look different from hitting a grand slam with your children. There is no cookie-cutter formula for success in all these areas.

What can we say about greatness, then? If there are so many different grand slams, does anything unite them?

Let me hazard a few principles to guide the chase for greatness.

First, the *chase* for greatness is almost as important as the "greatness" itself. Being truly great requires a burning desire to be great. We'll discuss this further as we get into the bases of the grand slam, but the great enemy of greatness is complacency. Being complacent, giving up the chase, and losing the burning desire, is a surefire way to avoid greatness and end up with a life full of regret. Any kind of grand slam requires the chase, the determination to achieve a goal, and the discipline necessary to get there.

Second, while there are objective qualities to greatness, on the whole, true greatness is defined by other people. You may have your own definition of what a great marriage looks like, for example. You may even have a burning desire to achieve it. You might even think you already have a great marriage. But if I ask your husband or wife and they say the marriage isn't so great...well, then the marriage isn't so great. You might think you're a great boss, but if your employees disagree, chances are there's something wrong with your leadership.

So intrinsic qualities certainly matter: things like integrity, kindness, honesty, and so on. These are essential in all of life's endeavors, and no grand slam can happen without them. To a large extent, greatness depends on the impact that your life has on others, and therefore on how others define what it means for you to be great in a particular area. Just like a grand slam with no one on base is simply a home run, "greatness" achieved alone isn't truly greatness.

Third, greatness is tied to vocation, and it requires the setting of priorities. Try as you might, you probably won't be able to hit a grand slam in every area of your life. A grand slam isn't a supernatural feat, it's a human one, done by limited human people. You are only one person, you only have so many hours in your day, days in your year, and years in your life. You can't expect yourself to achieve greatness in every area of life. But you can live up to your calling, your vocation, and you can chase greatness in that area.

Just think about all of the different grand slams we talked about. Many of these are lifetime achievements. They are the result of an entire life committed to greatness in one specific area. Greatness requires a measure of specialization, and specialization, by definition, is a narrowing of one's focus on a particular goal. Thankfully, many of the goals we set for our own lives do not exclude success in other areas by necessity in the way that being a professional basketball player excludes being a professional baseball player. But this doesn't mean that priorities aren't important.

What does this look like in practice? Well, let's say that you are committed to chasing greatness in your marriage and with your children. You want to be the best spouse and parent that you can be. For you, this might mean that at work, you have to settle for singles and doubles instead of a grand slam. Maybe this looks like not taking a promotion that's going to require more hours and more travel in order to prioritize making it to your daughter's soccer games or your son's school plays. Maybe it means being a bit less productive and not taking calls from clients after hours so that your husband knows that when you're home, he has your full attention. Maybe it looks like making less money now because time with your wife is actually more valuable than whatever luxuries that bump in pay might provide.

If this is how your priorities fall, I'm here

to tell you that is completely okay. In fact, that's what greatness looks like. It is chasing after what *you* value the most with clarity about the end goal. And prioritizing like this allows you to make sacrifices, even difficult ones, because you know that spending less time or effort in one area of your life is going to have amazing benefits in the areas you care about the most.

Grand slams are great, and we are all about them in this book, no doubt. But singles, doubles, and triples are nothing to shake a stick at. They're good. And it's okay if, in the course of your life, you look back and realize that like Derek Jeter you only hit one grand slam, as long as it was the one that was the most important to you and you truly chased greatness to achieve it.

Cooperstown

Cooperstown, New York is the home of the Baseball Hall of Fame. It is a kind of shrine to greatness, a place where people flock to encounter the all-time greats of the game. We're talking the Great Bambino, Joe Dimaggio, Ty Cobb, Mickey Mantle, Hank Aaron, Willie Mays, and hundreds more. These guys hit some serious grand slams and put together careers that have been memorialized for all time in Cooperstown. And yet, they still, for the most part, failed to reach base over two-thirds of the time! But nobody talks about the strikeouts or double plays they hit into. Instead, they are remembered for the great feats they accomplished on the field, for their consistency, for their performance in the big moments of games, for all the times they stepped back into the batter's box after a strikeout and did something amazing that lifted their teams, maybe even a grand slam.

Greatness doesn't mean that you'll never fail. Every single person in the Hall of Fame failed, and failed *more* than they succeeded. But what sets them apart is the way that they continued to be intense and disciplined, the way they continued to work with their teammates in the locker room. They continued to see pitches and to take the chances that were given to them.

Cooperstown isn't a home for perfection,

it's a home for greatness. And that's an important distinction.

So the batter's box represents the first step of the grand slam life. The grand slam starts and ends in the batter's box. It's the place where you make a commitment to changing your own life, but more importantly, to changing the lives of others. It's where you commit to leaving a legacy, to living a life that will be remembered by those that you've impacted. Every trip to the batter's box is a new opportunity, a chance to spit on complacency and chase greatness.

"EVERY TRIP TO THE BATTER'S BOX IS A NEW OPPORTUNITY, A CHANCE TO SPIT ON COMPLACENCY AND CHASE GREATNESS."

Base Study: The Batter's Box

Nico (14) | *Desoto, KS*

I've always loved baseball, ever since I was really young. I remember playing T-ball as a four-year-old. At a tournament one time, we ran into this guy who had a little bit of baseball knowledge at the professional level. So we started asking questions about how I could better myself as a player. At the time I was a catcher, hitting right-handed. My Dad asked what was the quickest way to get to the Major Leagues. The guy responded, "Become a switch-hitting catcher." So I started working on switch-hitting. Honestly, I was pretty bad for the first two years. I took more at-bats from the left side than the right side. I would just go lefty and work on it, but it felt like no progress, especially in games. I would go o for 4, game after game, and had very little success at the plate.

My Dad always wants me to be the best player that I can be, and he always supports me. He said that I had the option to quit trying and focus on improving as a right-handed hitter. But I told him I wanted to stay with it. I started getting better. I went to Damage Hitters to have hitting lessons with Coach Karl and I worked on hitting left-handed, and I just kept at it and kept improving.

I had a tournament in Illinois when I was 12. It was a competitive game, we were down by three, and I was up to bat. The bases were loaded with two outs and I was most definitely nervous, but just had to do my job. I stepped up to the left side of the plate and worked myself to a full count. The pitcher threw me a fastball like a beach ball and I put a really good swing on it. Off the bat, I didn't know it was going to be a home run. So I took off trying to get extra bases and as I was rounding first, my coach gave me a high-five. I realized I had just hit a grand slam from the left side! That was probably the happiest I've been playing baseball. It was such a magical experience; it was my first home run and it was a grand slam on the left side. It was extremely special for me. I can still hear my mom screaming from the stands.

I was able to keep going with switch-hitting because I just knew that even if it was hard in the moment, if I kept at it, it would make me a better player in the long run. And I really want to be a great baseball player.

For me, greatness is something that you have to strive towards. You don't just stumble upon greatness. You have to be intentional with every single aspect of your life.

— Nico Martinez, *Grand Slam: Determination*

Chapter 2
First Base

The 90 feet from the batter's box to first base is the most heavily trodden stretch on the ball diamond. Whether you just sent the ball 500 feet onto Waveland Avenue, or you laid down a bad bunt that popped straight to the pitcher, you still need to run to first base.

What's especially interesting about the first 90 feet of the base path is that typically the batter doesn't know exactly how the play is going to end when he starts toward first base. Is the bloop fly ball to shallow left field going to drop in for a hit? Is the shortstop going to fumble a routine ground ball that means you'll have a split second longer to make it to first? Can you beat out the throw from second to save an out on a double play? Is the deep fly ball going to hold up on the warning track or make it over the fence?

This split second of unpredictability is a kind of sacred moment in baseball. In the little eternity just after the ball flies off the bat, anything could happen. Fans could witness an incredible defensive play or an embarrassing error, a game-winning home run or a game-saving catch. And this beautiful chaos is based on the fundamental human limit of being time-bound. We cannot know the future; we aren't certain how things will play out. This is why any coach worth their salt will tell their players to bust it out of the batter's box in every situation, because they never know what will happen at the end of the play.

If you've ever watched a baseball game where the batter doesn't do this and pays the price, you know the frustration it creates in fans, coaches, and teammates. Not hustling to first can cost your team a crucial out, strand runners on base, and even lose your team the game. And what's more, it communicates something about the player. It suggests to everyone, even if it isn't entirely true, that he has better things to do, that he doesn't really care, and that he lacks commitment, both to his own greatness and to the team's success.

Your attitude toward first base is a microcosm of your attitude toward the entire game.

We've made it out of the batter's box and are heading to first, but before we dive into what first base represents for the grand slam life, I want to emphasize an important distinction between running bases and living the grand slam life: in baseball, you have to run the bases in order; in life, things are rarely linear. What this means for our purposes is simply that the grand slam life is not a four-step process to success in which you move from the batter's box to first, first to second, second to third, and check off each step as you do so. The life principles that are represented by each of the bases are interconnected and overlapping, not linear or mutually exclusive. We'll continue to draw this out as we move through the bases, but suffice it to say, we're talking less about steps and more about "bases" in the traditional meaning of the word: foundations—foundations on which to build a truly great life.

Intentionality

The attitude toward running to first that we just outlined can be summed up by a single word: *intentionality*. You can tell when someone takes off toward first base from the batter's box with intentionality and when they don't. You can see from the very first steps down the base path what the intention of the base runner is. Is she intending to make it to first base at all costs? Or is she just jogging down the baseline assuming that the defense won't make a play, or assuming she knows where the ball will fall?

The drive, the motivation, and the intent demonstrated by someone sprinting toward first base to see out the play is a picture of the intentionality necessary to live a truly great life, to hit a grand slam. Intentionality is the gun that sounds off the race. If you're intentional about doing something, you're hell-bent to get it done, and you're going to find a way to accomplish it. You set your mind to it and you orient all of yourself toward its accomplishment.

Being intentional is all-encompassing. To be intentional about hitting your grand slam, whatever that looks like for you, means aligning all of the elements of your life in service to that goal. The choices that you make, the routines and habits that you form, and the way you spend your money and your time, are all determined by your intention. When you live intentionally, you start to shape your life toward something, toward greatness.

I started seriously thinking about my life and developing a burning desire for greatness after attending the funeral of a co-worker. It was around the time my wife and I had our first child. I was traveling a lot with my job and working long hours. Sometimes my wife saw me, and sometimes she didn't. I was making good money, the most I had ever made in my life, in fact. I was providing for my family in a tangible way, creating a life that was comfortable and stable, and able to be generous with others. In the eyes of a lot of folks, I was immensely successful, perhaps even heading toward a kind of greatness.

But I was on the road often. And when my daughter was born, I realized that my priorities were shifting. My grand slam had changed. I wanted to be home. I wanted to be there, to be present. I wanted to change diapers. I wanted to let my wife sleep while I took care of the baby. In fact, I have a memory that is etched in my mind for life. My daughter was 6 days old and, as infants so often are, she was wide awake at 1:00 AM. I went to pick her up and she looked right into my eyes and her eyes said, "You are my Daddy." It was as if she actually verbalized those words. So I decided to step out of my role at work and move into more of a management role that didn't require quite as much travel and allowed me to reduce my time spent on the road. That was intentional. It was a conscious decision I made to change my role (thus reducing my earning potential) in order to prioritize my wife and my daughter.

Prioritizing is the key. As we discussed before, you can't be great in every area of your life, and that means you can't be equally intentional about everything. Intentionality assumes a destination and therefore a direction. You might be able to make a few stops or route yourself through some interesting towns along the way, but you can't end up in Los Angeles and Washington D.C. at the same time and through the same path.

So if you want to hit a grand slam, you need to start thinking seriously about your destination. What is greatness for you? What do you want to prioritize? What changes do you need to make? Once you know where you're going, you can start taking the intentional steps necessary to get there.

Fighting the Enemy: Complacency

Intentionality as I've been laying it out here can be elusive to describe, but it is conspicuous by its absence. Just as you only think about the umpire when he's making bad calls, you *really* notice intentionality when it's not there. When someone is living aimlessly, doesn't have clear priorities, and seems to dart about from one thing to another without ever actually doing anything, it is easy to see.

A life lived without intentionality ends up looking like a life just going through the motions. There is no zeal for improvement, no burning desire to impact those around you positively, and no vision for what your life could be. Or, in the words of my friend Josh, "Too much fake hustle." This not only robs you of experiencing the fullness of your own life, but also it deprives others of the person you have the potential to be. So if you lack intentionality in your marriage, for example, it isn't just you that will suffer, but your spouse as well, and likely even more. If you lack intentionality at work, your co-workers and business as a whole will feel the negative effects.

What we're talking about here, to put it simply, is *complacency*. It is satisfaction with a state of affairs in one's own life that stops short of greatness. It is making a concession to mediocrity. It is jogging to first base, assuming that the shortstop won't make the play.

If a burning desire for greatness is the beating heart of the grand slam life, complacency is a steady diet of cheeseburgers that clogs the arteries and keeps that heart from beating. Burning desire relishes opportunities. It takes advantage of each chance that it gets. It has a clear vision for the future and does whatever it can to get there. Complacency sees opportunities as a burden, or imagines that they will always be there. It sits out this round and assumes another one will come around. Its vision for the future looks a lot like today or yesterday, if it exists at all.

We talked about opportunity and failure in the previous chapter about the batter's box. And it's really important to be clear that failure and greatness are not mutually exclusive. Failure is part and parcel of greatness. I would go so far as to say that greatness is not possible without failure. Adversity and suffering are necessary parts of growing as a person, of maturing mentally and emotionally, and of developing the depth of personality and insight that we commonly call "wisdom." Failures, large and small, are unavoidable, and they are why opportunities are so important, why second chances matter so much. Truly great players keep getting back into the batter's box, and truly great lives are made by waking up and taking the opportunities of each new day, especially in the face of recent failure, suffering, and heartbreak.

The shadow side of second chances, however, is visible in the complacent life. Whereas the great life seizes each opportunity like it's the last one, complacency believes that there will always be another chance. The complacent batter says "I struck out this time? Oh well, there will be plenty of chances in the future." And while there is a time and a place for such an attitude, the complacent person never adjusts. And suddenly, the end of his baseball career arrives, and he realizes that his chances were not unlimited, that he may never step up to the plate again, and that he has wasted his career by never taking an opportunity to improve.

We see this all too often in the lives of those around us. Everyone knows someone with great potential who has just never made the most of their talents. Everyone knows someone limping along in a marriage or a job that could be so much more, but who just cannot be bothered to make any changes. Everyone knows someone who is estranged from a friend or child and insists that they'll get around to reconciling eventually.

What complacency obscures, then, is the basic fact of mortality. Our lives are limited. We don't have unlimited chances, and what's more, we aren't even promised tomorrow. But, like the rules of baseball, these limits don't have to be oppressive or debilitating. Instead, they can be the base (if you catch my drift) for a rich and fulfilling life, one that is truly great. They can spur incredible acts of kindness, self-sacrifice, love, and achievement simply by spurring us on to see our lives as they really are: a dash!

Few things are more deadly to complacency than recognizing our impermanence and our human limits. Few things are more motivating than knowing that the clock is running.

Now, what I'm not saying here is that life needs to be constant striving and that there is no place for contentment, rest, or even healthy pride in one's achievements. These are all healthy things and are in no way contradictory to the grand slam life. Contentment is a wonderful thing to aim for in life, and a great life will surely be one character- ized by contentment. But when contentment slips into complacency, that is, when you become satisfied with an unhealthy or medi- ocre state of affairs in your life, things need shaking up.

Avoiding Complacency: Hard Work and Self-Honesty

So how can we avoid complacency? What does intentionality require? There is much we could say here, but I want to focus on two things: working hard and being honest with oneself.

As we've already gestured towards, being intentional requires hard work. Intentionality necessitates planning and premeditation, a strategy to allow you to reach a vision. And this can be daunting. Stepping back and making a plan for your life is not easy. The busyness of daily life often makes us feel that we must focus on what is urgent, regardless of how important it is. But a true burning desire for greatness will be laser-focused on the goal, and make the time to plan and prepare a path to get there.

Beyond simply the hard work of planning is the hard work of following through. This is where the rubber meets the road. It's where burning desire turns into action, muscling through the challenges each day presents on the road to greatness. This is where you will feel the sacrifices, the pain of priorities, and the self-denial necessary to achieve your goals. And hitting your grand slam means pushing through all of that to reap the rewards on the other side.

Second, intentionality requires us to be honest with ourselves. It means taking a hard look at our own lives and admitting what needs to change. It means recognizing where we are falling short and committing to improving in those areas. And it means overcoming the common lies that we tell ourselves about what we can and cannot do.

There are two ways we deceive ourselves. One, we overestimate our ability. We imagine that perfection is possible and get hung up on failures that prevent us from getting back into the batter's box. The lie of "perfection" keeps us from seeing failure as part of a larger process. <u>We overestimate our ability to be perfect in the moment and not see that what we are really aiming for is growth</u>. This is why the *chase* for greatness is so important. It may be the case that you never achieve the high standards that you set for greatness, but there is a sense in which greatness is more of a journey than a destination.

Two, we often underestimate ourselves. We look at the task ahead of us, the grand slam that we want to hit, and we think it's just too tall of an order. That fence is really far away. How could I possibly hit a ball over it? And with all the pressure of three runners on base to boot? And so maybe we don't even try. We fall into despair and think we just can't do it. We can never really change, we could never be truly great.

I'm here to tell you that you need to silence these voices in your head. Stop believing the lies. Be honest with yourself. You don't need to be perfect, and you *can* really change. Your failures don't define you, and you *can* become the person you were meant to be. That is what hitting your grand slam is all about. That's the thrill of the chase. So choose intentionality, set your priorities, and bust it down the first base line. You're already on your way.

Mark A. Martinez

Base Study: First Base

GUENTHER DZIUVENIS (69) | *SCOTTSDALE, AZ*

In 2007, I was diagnosed with kidney cancer. Kidney cancer is a silent but serious type of cancer. Usually, by the time you realize you have it, it's too late. In my situation, not only was I diagnosed with kidney cancer, but it had already metastasized to my lungs. I had hundreds of tumors in my lungs which made it inoperable. The way I found out I had it was I was on a business trip to Seattle. I had come down with a chronic cough that I just couldn't shake. I'd been there all week and on Friday night was heading back home. I called my wife and asked if she could schedule an appointment with our doctor because I needed to get some antibiotics to get rid of this cough. When I visited, the doctor listened to my lungs, agreed that I probably needed some antibiotics, and wrote the prescription. As I was getting ready to leave with the prescription in hand, she turned to me and asked, "Guenther, when was the last time you had a chest x-ray?" After a long week, I had no desire to stay for another hour for a chest x-ray. I started to walk out the door, but she was adamant, so I acquiesced.

Monday morning, at 7AM, I got a call from the doctor's office asking me to come in to talk about the x-ray. Long story short, she said to me, "I think you have kidney cancer." I was shocked. I couldn't believe it. *Kidney cancer.* The cancer in my lungs had started to bleed. By that point, it's usually too late.

So I went to see oncologists and they told me that they couldn't do surgery because my lungs were full of tumors. They said they wanted to try a new treatment called Interleukin-2, administered via drip bags in the ICU, which would make me extremely sick. Essentially they would take me as close to death as possible with the hope that my immune system would kick in and fight the cancer. There was no guarantee that this would work. I'd go into the ICU, spend 4 to 5 days getting the treatment, go home and recover, and then go back into the ICU two weeks later. The plan was to do that eight times. The pain of the treatments was immense. After one visit I remember commenting that it was how I imagined torture.

After my third visit, the oncologist came into my room with x-ray in hand and said something like, "Guenther, what would you do if I told you that we can no longer see any tumors in your lungs?" I replied, "I'd probably start to cry." He responded, "Well, you better start crying."

The treatment was working, but I had to continue with the rest of the visits. So I did the eight treatments over a period of six months. I survived. When I first started, they told me there was a 50/50 chance of survival. It was only after I was finally cleared that they told me the survival rate was more like 17% in my situation.

In this process of going through months of cancer treatments, intentionality was critical. When you are diagnosed with late-stage cancer, you have two choices. You can either give up, or you can be intentional and try to survive. Intentionality became my theme, and I got better and better one day at a time. Every day I would wake up and praise the Lord that I woke up. From there I would think about how I was going to maximize my time that day and make sure I was doing things in a way that would make me healthier. A big part of that was trying to maintain a positive attitude. Another part of that was making sure I slept well every night and ate well every day. I even had a colleague that would text me every morning the words, "Better and better every day."

While I was somewhat afraid of dying, what troubled me more was the thought of leaving behind a family that needed me. So my focus was on survival more for them than for me.

Life throws challenges at all of us. I'm a big college football fan, and the famous coach, Lou Holtz, always says, "It's not what happens to you, it's how you react to what happens to you." I truly believe that. In life, if you aren't intentional in addressing the challenge or issue head-on, you're not likely to succeed. I think that's at the heart of Mark's message, and what got me through cancer. It was trying to get better and better every day until the cancer was gone. And eventually, it was.

— Guenther Dziuvenis, *Grand Slam: Beat Cancer*

Chapter 3
Second Base

You're rounding first and you've been sprinting with your head down, looking up just in time to see the ball land on the other side of the fence. As your pace slows to a trot and you begin to enjoy your romp around the bases, you have the time to look around a bit and enjoy the view. Maybe you notice the fans chanting your name in ecstasy, sending the decibel level in the stadium through the roof. Maybe you know where your kids are sitting and you give them a wave and a wink.

Eventually, however, you would look over to see your teammates running ahead of you, the guys whose presence on base made your home run maximally valuable. They are the reason the crowd is awestruck by your home run, why what the fans just witnessed is more than just a routine home run. Those baserunners—the same people that were in the locker room with you before the game and who will be there afterward—are integral to your grand slam. In fact, there is no grand slam without them. And the beautiful thing is, because they are on your team, they not only contribute to your grand slam, they benefit from it. The runs go on the scoreboard for the team, not just for you.

This is what second base of the grand slam life is all about: community. It's about the people who impact you, who help you along your chase for greatness. But it's also about the people that you impact, the beneficiaries of the greatness you achieve in your own life. No one hits a grand slam alone, and no one lives a truly great life alone. So anyone chasing greatness needs to ask: who's on first?

Who's on first? The difference between a grand slam and a solo shot

What is the basic difference between a grand slam and a solo home run? Why should a grand slam be worth four times as much as a solo shot? Well, remember those statistics about the typical batting average for a Major League hitter? We've talked about the frequency of failure in baseball. If the average hitter reaches base only once every four times they step up to the plate (a .250 average), then the likelihood of three players reaching base consecutively is less than 2%. That means that by the time you step into the box with the bases loaded, you're already dealing with a rare situation in which each person before you has beaten the odds to reach base. They have put in the work to make sure that you have this opportunity. And there's no guarantee, with how unlikely the situation is, that you'll get the same chance again.

So of course a grand slam should be worth four times as much as a solo home run. It requires the efforts of four people, and is far, far less likely to happen than a solo home run is. <u>A grand slam is a team effort.</u> The home run hitter might get all the credit and be remembered, but his achievement would be peanuts without the hard work, determination, and support of his teammates who reached base before him and presented him with the chance to do something truly great.

As in baseball, so in life: the grand slam cannot happen alone. The truly great life is impossible without the contributions of key members of one's life. Whether it be a parent, a mentor, a spouse, a friend, a child, or any number of other relationships in your life, you can't get where you want to go alone.

Many people in our modern Western society, and especially in the United States, still hold on to the myth of the self-made man or woman. The cultural fiction of the bootstrapping individual who against all odds makes something out of nothing without the help of anyone or anything holds a strong sway over the American imagination. We prefer to believe that we have earned everything we have on the basis of our own merit, skill, and hard work. We don't like to be dependent upon other people, and we generally hate owing anything to anybody. While many of us might enjoy *giving* help to other people in need, far fewer of us enjoy *receiving* help, and an even smaller number would ever consider actually asking for it.

There are a variety of historical and cultural reasons for this very American disposition, but for our purposes what is needed most here is that self-honesty we talked about as a necessary ingredient for intentionality. Whoever you are, and however impressive you are, you are not an island. You are not a self-made individual. You did not spring up, unbidden from the dirt, and create success for yourself with a little elbow grease. Admitting this is the first step.

This is not at all to say that individuals can't work hard or earn things, or that there aren't people who have overcome staggering odds to get to where they are in life. Far from it! The grand slam life is built on the idea that it's possible to go from mediocrity to greatness and to overcome challenges that seem insurmountable at first glance. It is simply to say that no one truly does this alone. There might be a solo home run in baseball, but I don't think there is such a thing in life.

The reason for this isn't that humans are weak or incapable. It's because we are human. And to be human is to be a creature who thrives in community and withers in isolation. Think about human babies, for example. While some species of animals can abandon their young almost immediately to fend for themselves, if humans abandon our young and no one steps in, there is no hope for survival. From our earliest stage, we are dependent upon others for our very lives.

As we grow older and develop, it can be tempting to believe the illusion that we cease depending on others, that we exit the network of formative and necessary human relation- ships. But this is simply not the case. Our parents, our friends and co-workers, our spouses, these relationships, and others much more superficial, continue to form the basis of our personal and psychological development. We need others to be ourselves.

The grand slam life will acknowledge this early and often. No greatness is purely indi- vidual. Humans cannot do hard things alone.

We need some sort of motivation, some kind of story or context that makes sense of our chase for greatness, that defines what greatness really is for us. You will never get back into the batter's box if your only motivation for getting a hit is yourself. And even if you do, you'll realize that the most you can do alone is score a single run, and that's not going to cut it for the vast majority of games.

Chasing greatness happens with others and because of others. Chase alone, and you'll run out of gas before you even get close.

In practical terms, this means you need to surround yourself with a good team. Greatness depends upon mentors, trainers, coaches, wise elders, and communities of support. It depends upon *friendship*, on a locker room full of trusted companions.

This is a simple but radical notion in our current context. The observation that we are more connected than ever and yet more isolated than ever has become a cliché, but clichés become clichés for a reason. Too many people, and especially men, have no real community to speak of, no real friends. Too many have bought into the lie that greatness means flying solo and not asking for help. Vulnerability is seen as weakness, and building real relationships with others is seen as an untenable risk or an unthinkable chore. As a result, many of us are living lives starved of real connection and relationship with others.

To this, the grand slam life says: YES. Real connection with others, real friendship, is the foundation of greatness. Loneliness and isolation are great ways to kill a grand slam before it starts. You just can't do it alone. You likely already have a community surrounding you that informs what your grand slam looks like. And you also probably have people in your life that have formed and shaped you into the person you are today, with all your gifts, passions, and personality. Chasing greatness means drawing on these relationships and cultivating them. It means being nourished by deep friendships characterized by vulnerability and honesty. The grand slam is a long haul, it's the work of a life. <u>Soaking up the encouragement and support of friends and family is absolutely essential</u>. Remember: life is a team sport.

Winning for the Team

Some of the most admired baseball players in the history of the game are beloved not just for their star quality and their outstanding talent, but because they were what we often call "team players." A team player isn't necessarily the most gifted player on the team, and he may not be the flashiest or have the most personality. Team players are typically celebrated for their willingness to give everything they have for the success of the team, their ability to keep the ultimate goal of winning as a team above their own stat sheet. They don't live for the spotlight, but they will step up in big moments because of their commitment to the team.

Why do we find these players so compelling? What is so captivating about a team player if it isn't their raw talent or star power? I think team players speak to a deeply felt notion that our success should be *for others*. They embody a kind of attainable version of greatness. There will probably always be someone more talented than me at whatever it is that I do. I'll never be the

number one ranked *anything*. The thing
about rare talents is that they are, well, *rare*.
But a team player? Now that's something I
can aspire to be, that's something I can
reasonably achieve. I can be the guy who my
team can count on, a guy who plays an important role, a guy who puts the good of the
group before my individual stats. That
doesn't take the most talent, it just takes a
humble heart and a clear vision of success.

The team player is a good image for the
way a grand slam requires others: real greatness is greatness *for others*. We've noted this
before: true greatness is measured by others
as well as yourself. You need others not only
as a means to help you hit a grand slam, but
also as the purpose for the grand slam itself.
The grand slam life is devoted to impacting
others, just as it needs others to be possible in
the first place.

I've mentioned this before, but I think it's
worth saying again here in a slightly different
key: *no one does hard things alone*. Think
about the things that motivate you the most in
life. I'd imagine that at least some of the
things that come to mind are actually other

people, perhaps kids, your spouse, your family or friends, or others.

As a dad, it's hard not to default to fatherhood to illustrate the point. There's a genre of clickbait-style articles that capture what I'm getting at perfectly, and they're typically titled something like "Hero Dad Lifts Car to Save Child" or "Super Dad Runs 20 Miles to Hail Doctor for Injured Son" or "Father Slam Dunks Basketball from Half Court to Save Cartoons from Alien Space Prison." Okay, that last one is actually the plot of the original *Space Jam*, but that movie is also kind of a perfect illustration of this idea so we're going to forge ahead.

The basic structure of these stories is that a dad (or perhaps even more often, a mom) performs some feat of superhuman ability to save his or her child from serious danger. In Michael Jordan's case, this was stretching his arms to about twenty times their normal length. In the real-world cases above, it often results in a moment of incredible strength, speed, or stamina. What is so incredible about these stories is that they have basically nothing to do with the parent doing the saving. In fact, what makes them remarkable is that the dad or mom is usually just an ordinary, unassuming parent, not a bodybuilder or pro athlete or Navy Seal. The miraculous act is enabled entirely by the child, because it is done on the child's behalf. It is the motivation of love for the child that powers the strength or speed, not anything specific about the parent. And these stories connect with us on such a deep level because most of us know exactly what it is like to love someone so much that you could lift a car or run 20 miles to save them.

Motivation like this sits at the heart of the grand slam life and distinguishes it from a life of solo home runs. Truly great lives are lived for others, and the others for which we live give us the strength to endure exhaustion, hardship, and suffering beyond what we would ever be capable of alone. The way your life can impact and change the lives of others for the better fans the flame of your burning desire for greatness and gives you the fuel you need for the chase. So whatever your grand slam looks like, you need to ask yourself: who is this for, and how will it affect their lives? A true grand slam will have a clear answer to that question and will draw motivation from it.

It takes three

A grand slam in baseball is impossible without three batters who have already gotten on base. For a true grand slam, you need others. What kinds of traits foster healthy community? How can you make the most of your baserunners? Well, remember all that talk about the locker room at the very beginning of the book? Here, at second base, is where what happens in the locker room becomes concrete on the basepaths.

I've worked with a lot of guys in my life in various circles, and have met with a particular group of men from my church for over ten years running. We've created this environment where men walk into the room, and, just like they would in a locker room, they're willing to strip down and bare all of their issues and challenges in the midst of other men. This doesn't happen overnight, to be sure. It comes about over time. But the reason why the men in this group are willing to do that is because there's *trust*. Vulnerability cannot exist without trust, and if you don't have a circle of trusted friends or family, people who can really see and speak into your life, your grand slam journey is going to be a whole lot more difficult. I don't mean to say you should naively allow anyone into the most sacred and profound parts of your life. There is much wisdom in being cautious about how much we share about our lives, and with whom we share. Being burned hurts, and when trust is broken, it's extremely difficult to repair.

That being said, relationships require risk, and the only way to insulate yourself from pain caused by others is to totally isolate yourself, and isolation makes grand slams impossible. Grand slams are hit with a team, and to get the most out of your team, you need to foster an environment where you can be open with others, especially about fears and failures. There are few things more encouraging or more powerful for self-confidence and self-esteem than for someone to see all the really messed-up parts of your life and say, "I love you anyway."

To stick with the image of the locker for a moment, I like to imagine that classic high school locker with the little vents at the top. You know the one. Just thinking about it probably brings a certain...aroma to mind. Those three little vents towards the top exist so that air can circulate and prevent moldy, smelly death from consuming the whole locker. I don't know about you, but in my experience, they aren't very good at their job. In fact, they often do a better job of spreading odor than preventing it.

Our own inner lives can be a lot like that smelly, moldy locker. When you aren't vulnerable, when your locker door is closed, there's no light and very little air getting into your locker. Your shoes, your sweaty practice gear, and last week's lunch, all start to stink, and then they start to fester, and all of a sudden they are glowing a radioactive green and are housing a family of those little gremlins from the toe fungus commercials. The impulse here is to double down and keep the locker shut up tight. But you are fooling yourself to think that the stench from the challenges that you're dealing with is not coming through the vents of that locker and stinking up your interactions with other people.

What you really need, counterintuitively, is to open that nasty locker and expose it to light and air. Because when that locker door opens, you realize that guy or gal who has the locker next to you has some of the very same issues, or has achieved success in some of those same areas. You realize that you're better off with that door as wide open as possible because others can come in and help. You can get the dirty laundry out to the washing machine, let your sweaty shoes dry, and toss that three-week-old ham sandwich in the trash.

Opening up your locker is crucial for allowing others to come alongside you in your grand slam journey, because those same people who see your locker are going to be the ones on base when you step up to the plate. And the stronger those relationships are, the more vulnerability and accountability you foster, the better your chances of hitting a grand slam.

This is true in all areas of life. It's almost self-evident in personal relationships, but it holds for corporate environments as well. In a corporate environment, vulnerability needs to start at the leadership level. From there it filters down to the employee and into personal relationships. Vulnerability is mutually shared and mutually owned. A key way this plays out in a corporate context is openness to feedback. There's a vulnerability that comes with opening yourself up to criticism, and a leader who models that is going to create a culture where feedback is a positive thing and can sharpen everyone. If the leader models receiving feedback and criticism, then you can expect the employees to do that as well.

Few of us start in brand-new locker rooms. Sometimes you get a locker that's old, moldy, and rusty. Maybe there's some unknown residue in the corner. Dealing with these pre-existing issues can be extremely difficult. But it's important to know that your locker doesn't have to stay the way it was when you inherited it. You can clean out your locker, open it up, expose it to the light, and ask others for help. Or you can keep it closed and risk the mold spreading if it's not tended to. Let's change so the next generation starts with less stuff in their locker.

Worms

I love worms. We live in a rural area outside Kansas City. On days that we get a lot of rain, the water tends to push the worms out of the soil and into the street. And if you've ever seen a worm on asphalt, you've seen it squirming and moving and trying to do everything it can to survive long enough to get back to the soil. My wife and I love to go on walks after it has just rained, and there's a spot on our walk where there tends to be an abundance of worms after a good storm. And, being a bit weird, what I always do on these walks is pick up worms. I pick them up and toss them back onto the soil.

As I was doing this one time, it dawned on me that that worm, writhing and fighting for its life on the sidewalk, is no different than the people that you and I come across in our everyday lives. Many folks are struggling to get through whatever challenges they are facing in their lives. They're struggling to get back to a spot where they're thriving and being nourished in a healthy environment. And while they may not be wiggling around prostrate on wet concrete (though you never know what rock bottom might look like for a given person), they are a lot like that worm. They're fighting, they're wrestling, they're uncomfortable, and they're not satisfied with life.

And like the rain for the worms, for many people something in their life has caused them to be in a spot where they're uncomfortable and unhappy with their circumstances. That could be any number of things. Often it's self-inflicted, the loss of a job because of indiscretion, or broken relationships because of selfishness or carelessness. Perhaps even more often it's a situation beyond anyone's control—grief over the loss of a loved one, unexpected job loss, or chronic illness. Whatever the cause, in these difficult moments in our lives we end up looking a lot like beached worms.

What do worms have to do with second

base, or with the grand slam at all? Well, other than the off chance that you might encounter a real worm lying on the basepath, picking up worms is a simple picture of what the greatness of a grand slam life can look like. Chasing greatness isn't a blind march toward your goal with no concern for the people you encounter along the way. It isn't ignoring everyone else around you to find success. Grand slams are hit for others, not just for ourselves. So chasing greatness can look like stopping to pick up worms, and tossing them back into the soil where they can thrive.

My job? Your job? It's picking up worms. I'm convinced that we come across those people in our lives in order to pick them up. This might look like helping someone pay their next utility bill. Maybe you need to loan someone one of the four cars sitting in your garage because they need transportation to get to work. We cross the paths of people in need of our help in life for a reason.

Now, I'm not suggesting that we need to develop savior complexes or imagine that we can rescue every person in need that we come across in our lives. If I spent my whole walk picking up every worm I saw and throwing it back into the dirt, it would take me hours to get just a few blocks. We can only do what we are capable of, and the outcome of a worm's life isn't in our hands simply because we stop to pick it up and toss it back onto soil. But it is up to us to do our part in others' journeys back to a better state, so a truly great life will be a bit messy. It's slimy. You'll get enmeshed in other people's problems. Your mental and emotional space will get taken up by issues that others are dealing with. You'll carry the weight of their burdens as a part of the weight that you carry with your own. This is what being intentional (first base) about others (second base) looks like. But if you want your life to be defined by chasing this grand slam and you're willing to go through the effort to pick up those worms, you'll be well on your way to greatness. And who knows, you may find that one day you're the worm, and you'll need someone to pick you up and return you to soil. So if you want to hit that grand slam, prepare to get some dirt on your fingers. Besides, a little grit will help you grip the bat.

Base Study: Second Base

STEVEN McCLELLAND (71) |
EDMOND, OK

I met my friend Pernell when I started as a technician at the University of Central Oklahoma. He quickly became my most valuable teammate. We became friends because he was a veteran of the Army, and I was a veteran of the Marine Corps. We were both Christians, so we hit it off. Two and a half years later an outside company partnered with the university to manage our department. They put together a team, which included myself, and a couple of other guys. Pernell was one of the employees let go in the process. The very next day, Pernell was intentional and went down to the new company's office to apply for a job. It was pretty remarkable that he essentially got his old job back. That was when we became even closer friends because we were both technicians and were working together regularly. Pernell was a good resource for things at the college. He'd been working there, his wife worked there, and his daughter worked there, so a lot of people knew him. He was just one of those likable guys. Anything you wanted or needed, he was willing to do it.

And then he had a nasty accident. His car flipped and he suffered a major head injury. From that point, it only went downhill for him. He lasted about a year, or maybe a year and a half after the accident. But in the 20 years that I knew the man, he was unselfish and willing to do whatever he could to help you. He was the perfect example of a great teammate. At his funeral, many people came and shared stories about how he positively impacted their lives and how he always put others first. Years later people still tell Pernell stories. I really, really miss Pernell and strive to model his behaviors every day.

— Steven McClelland, *Grand Slam: Servanthood*

Chapter 4
Third Base

Okay. You're rounding second and heading for third. You are officially over halfway around the bases, and with every step, there is far more basepath behind you than before you. It dawns on you that this trot around the bases will not last forever. The end is in sight, and you can see the players leaving the dugout to greet you at home plate. You've been celebrating on the basepath, soaking up the roar of the crowd, basking in the elation of the fans. Now you're faced with the fact that this journey is almost over, and it will only live on as a memory. Are you proud of the way you've run the bases? Do you have regrets?

Most people understandably want to beat

around the bush when it comes to the central theme of this chapter, but I think it's best just to say it up front: you're going to die. I've made a lot of claims in this book so far, a few promises, and a couple of predictions, but for this one, I'm going to give a guarantee: no matter who you are or how much money or power or fame you've accumulated in your life, you, reader, are going to die someday. And actually, you're dying right now. Every day, we all move a little closer to our deaths and get closer to the end of our timeline on this big blue ball.

I can hear some of you already saying, "This isn't news, of course I'm going to die." Cognitively, and intellectually, most of us are indeed aware of this. You know that humans don't live forever, and you are a human, so you put two and two together and get death. Simple. Factual. Obvious, even.

But here's the rub. Even though we all know on a basic level that we are going to die someday, most of us "know" it in the same way that we know Paris is the capital of France, or that birds have hollow bones, or that people who say they like turkey for

Thanksgiving dinner are lying. (Okay that last one is sort of my own opinion, but if you search yourself, I think you'll realize that it's also a fact.) These are the kinds of facts that we know in a way that has little impact on our lives. Paris being the capital of France doesn't really impact my daily life outside Kansas City. Birds having hollow bones is interesting trivia, but unless I'm a vet or a professional bird lifter it won't make much of a difference to me one way or the other. I know I'm eating turkey every Thanksgiving for the rest of my life, but it's still a bit surprising how mediocre even a well-cooked turkey can be. In each of these cases, the knowledge of a fact doesn't change how I live today; on the contrary, it's almost entirely irrelevant. There may be a moment where this knowledge will become helpful, to be sure, but in most situations and on 99.9% of days, it makes no difference at all.

This is how most of us treat the fact of our mortality. We know we are going to die eventually, but that fact has no visible impact on how we live in the present. And when death comes for us or the ones we love, we almost always respond with shock. How often have you heard something along the lines of "I just can't believe they're gone," "I thought we would have more time," or "If I would have known they were going to die, I would have done x, y, or z...?" I don't mean to belittle the seriousness of death or to suggest that death cannot be a shock. It certainly can. And death is certainly a cause for grief and sadness. To be parted from the ones that we love will never be easy, no matter how ready we think we might be. I'm simply illustrating the point that we can talk a big game about knowing that we'll die someday, but for most people in our culture, death, even a death we've been expecting for a long time, comes as a surprise.

To be fair, it is understandable that we respond like this, at least in our contemporary culture. We live in a society that is obsessed with youth and youthfulness. There are entire industries (arguably the majority of commercial industries) built on perpetuating the myth of eternal youth and immortality. Fashion, makeup, fitness and wellness, athletics, automobiles, and increasingly medicine— basically anything we use to curate an external image—serves to lift up the ideal of youthfulness and hide the reality of aging and the inevitability of death. You simply don't see many folks over 50 years old in advertising material or on television, unless the ads are explicitly targeting an older population. And when you do see elderly folks on television or in magazines, they rarely look their age. Gray hair, wrinkled skin, age spots, and the many other traditional markers of age are now easily taken care of by cosmetic treatments and procedures (of skyrocketing popularity, even among people in their twenties) that can convincingly erase physical signs of age.

I don't mean to pass any judgment here on the choices that individuals make about their appearance as they age. The desires to feel good and to look good are natural. I merely want to point out that in our day and age, feeling and looking good for many folks actually means feeling and looking *young*. And this makes aging, and reflecting on the reality of aging and mortality, all the more difficult because it becomes a sort of taboo, even embarrassing for people, as if it doesn't happen to every single person who has ever lived, including George Clooney.

Living Your Dash

So we're all going to die, and we all know it, but we all pretend like it's never going to happen, and so on a deeper level, we don't really know it. Why does this matter, what does it have to do with greatness, and what can be done about it? What's up with the suddenly super morbid subject matter? You thought this was a book about living your life to the fullest, and now I'm throwing you off by spending all this time talking about death. What gives?!

If you've made it this far, I can tell you the secret of third base, the crucial third element to greatness that all this melancholy has been building toward.

You can't hit a grand slam without living your dash.

Yes, you read that right: your dash. Let me explain.

First, let me just make a plug for strolling through cemeteries. Again, I know it might seem morbid, but if you live near a cemetery, take advantage of it. Few things in the world are a better reminder of the limits of our lives than cemeteries.

I realize it's not that common for folks to walk through cemeteries anymore, but headstones are still a familiar enough image that even if you don't spend much time in cemeteries (which you should!), you can picture the classic headstone format. Typically, a headstone includes the name of the person buried below it, perhaps with a verse of Scripture or a line from a poem, and then, typically in large print, there are two numbers, separated by, you guessed it, a *dash*. These two numbers are the year of the deceased's birth and death, two moments in time. And everything, every single day, every accomplishment, every disappointment, every insignificant blip and unforgettable bloop, *everything* that makes up that person's life, is represented by the dash in between those two numbers. An entire life summed up in an inch.

There's something incredibly appropriate about the shortness. Your life, my life, all of our lives, in the grand scheme of the universe, in the whole history of humankind, they are about an inch long. They are the blink of an eye. They are here today and gone tomorrow. You've heard that life is short, the dash says yes, about the width of your finger, in fact.

The dash, at its core, poses the question: do you realize that you don't have a whole lot of time left? Again, this isn't about being morbid or sad or discouraging. It's about telling the truth and facing up to reality: you don't have a lot of time, and you're closer to death today than you were yesterday. What are you going to do about it?

Living your dash means realizing you're sitting between those two dates, your birth and your death. And it means living each day with one eye on both of those dates, looking back toward the first and reflecting on the life you've lived, and looking forward to the second and preparing for the life you have left. The dash signifies the shortness of life and reminds us that we don't have long, but we do still have time left. We have time to right the wrongs of our past, and to live the best future we can. To put it another way, we are still in the middle of the chase for greatness. And the clock is ticking.

Regret and Forgiveness

Let's start with the first part of the dash: looking back. Some of us will look back on our lives largely with pride as we see fruitful marriages, well-adjusted adult children, long and prosperous careers, and healthy bank accounts well-positioned for retirement. There is much to be celebrated about a life well-lived, and there's nothing wrong with taking healthy pride in the blessings of one's life. But I'd wager that when most of us look back on our lives, we are less focused on our sterling slew of wins, and instead, our minds drift to those things we wish we would have done differently. To return to baseball, we look back and see strikeouts, bad at-bats, moments where the team needed a hit and we didn't deliver, and errors that cost our team a game.

What I want to say first is that this is completely normal. We've talked about failure quite a bit already, and it's important to say again: everyone fails, everyone messes up, and everyone wishes they could go back and do things differently. Everyone has regrets. It's normal, and it's okay. It's okay to look back and realize you didn't get everything right, that you struck out. Maybe you've had a marriage end in a messy and painful divorce. Maybe you missed out on a dream career opportunity or lost a job that you loved because of your own bad decision. Maybe you didn't have your priorities straight, and you missed out on important moments in your kids' lives or in other significant relationships because you just weren't around. Maybe you're staring at retirement with an empty bank account. Maybe you spent all your time and effort building something that has totally collapsed, and you'd do anything to go back and change it. Perhaps you are finishing high school or college and realizing that the dream of playing Major League Baseball has passed because you didn't commit to the grind required to be bigger, faster, and stronger.

Whatever it is, however big or small, regret is real. Mistakes were made...by all of us. Living your dash means looking back at your regrets and recognizing that they don't define you. When it comes to regrets and mistakes that we've made in the past, we need to do two primary things: change what we can, and forgive ourselves for what we can't.

First, when you live your dash to the fullest, you'll look for ways the past mistakes impact your present, and you'll try to repair everything that you possibly can. This is where intentionality and complacency come to mind, where you go back to first base. When you realize your life is short, that it's just a dash, you realize that you don't have unlimited time to repair what you've broken in your past. <u>Of course you won't be able to undo all the damage that you've caused in your life</u>, <u>but some things are most certainly reparable.</u> Broken relationships can be reconciled, pain can fade and healing can be found, enemies can become friends, and forgiveness is possible. Part of chasing greatness, part of living your dash, is acknowledging where you've failed and asking for forgiveness. It's apologizing and taking responsibility, responding to failure with humility rather

Do THIS Now!

than doubling down. These are hard things to do. They require swallowing our pride and admitting where we are wrong, that we did something bad, and that something is actually *my fault*.

The bright side of this is recognizing that while we can't undo the bad things we've done, we can make amends in many cases. Wounds can heal, even if they leave scars. A strikeout doesn't have to be your last at-bat.

Second, when you live your dash to the fullest, and you reflect on your past, you'll find that there are indeed things you can't change. Sometimes, there are wounds that can't be healed and relationships that can't be mended, no matter how hard we try. In these cases, forgiveness remains important, but it is self-forgiveness that is needed. When you've apologized where necessary, and made all the amends you can, you need to find a way to forgive yourself for the mistakes you've made in the past. While your past is a part of you, failures and all, it does not have to define you. It is how you live today that remains important, and dwelling endlessly on the mistakes of yesterday, especially if those mistakes are stopping you from chasing greatness, will only hold you back. <u>You've got to have</u> <u>compassion for yourself along with others.</u> <u>So</u> <u>forgive yourself, let others forgive you, and</u> <u>keep living</u>!

Let me give you a small but significant example from my own life. When my daughter was a month old, we decided to go to the mall. We parked, unloaded all the baby paraphernalia, and transferred her from the car to the stroller. Just like most new parents, we were sticklers for safety. I mean we drove the speed limit, washed her clothes in hypoallergenic detergent, and boiled the binky if it hit the ground. We were *those* parents. But on this particular day, I made a mistake.

As my wife fiddled with the 5-point harness that was meant to secure our precious cargo inside the Graco, I told her not to bother. I would take her out and hold her as soon as we got inside. She was skeptical, but complied. All was fine until we approached the curb. My wife needed to tilt the stroller down in order to lift the front wheels to clear the curb. When she did, our baby rolled out of her snug cocoon, and onto the asphalt. It all happened so fast. I scooped her up; there was blood on her head. How could I have done such a thing? Have I permanently injured her? Will she (and my wife) ever forgive me? Luckily, there was a nurse in the parking lot on her way in to shop. She saw the whole thing and rushed to help. After a cursory examination, she advised us to take her to a hospital. My mother-in-law, Mary, was behind the wheel. I don't even remember the race to the emergency room, but I know we exceeded the speed limit that time. Two hours, an x-ray, and lots of tears later we left with our sweet girl and the assurance that no long-term damage had been done. The blood we saw earlier was the result of a small scratch, no stitches needed.

We've shared that story with her, and I share it with you now to acknowledge I made a bad decision, a mistake. It's a moment I'm not proud of. It's a regret that I can't erase. Self-compassion and forgiveness from my wife have helped. What matters in the long run isn't that moment, it's how I've gone about tending to my daughter's welfare ever since. The type of father I want to be each day is one who owns up to mistakes, and asks for forgiveness when he messes up. My success as a father isn't defined by my worst moments, because I haven't let them be. I get to live my dash with my daughter every day.

Here is where the dash becomes especially helpful—it is a reminder that you still have time left to decide how you want your life to be defined, even if you don't know how much. You can still chase greatness. Get back into the batter's box. On the one hand, the dash is a sobering reminder that our time is limited, on the other it is a kick in the pants—get moving, you still have time before that second date on your tombstone!

Call to Action

We've spent time looking at the left side of the dash, but what about looking ahead to the second date, to the end? No one really knows when they're going to die, so why worry about the second date on the tombstone before it gets here? Well, in one sense, this question demonstrates a healthy posture towards death —since we can't know when we're going to die, we shouldn't spend a lot of time fretting about when it will be. And we certainly shouldn't live in fear of our death; it's a part of reality that we need to come to terms with.

But on the other hand, keeping that second date in the back of our minds really should change how we live. It is a constant reminder that we are not promised forever, and that we need to live the lives that we have now to the best of our ability. In baseball terms, it's the end of our last contract, our retirement date, the final at-bat. We've stressed that our lives are full of second chances, full of opportunities to get back into the batter's box, and that's very true. But it's also true that eventually you will have your last at-bat, your last chance for a grand slam. That fact isn't a cause for us to live in dread; rather, it's an encouragement and motivation to take every pitch we see seriously, and to grind out every at-bat that we get. The dash says that the secret to a good life is dying well, because if we live with the end in mind our lives will be better for it.

So I want to ask you directly now: what is your grand slam? Where do you have a burning desire to be great? Do you know? Have you thought about it? What are your beliefs about eternity? What areas of your life need more intentionality, more focus given to others? How can you live your dash? Because even though the days and the weeks can seem long, your life is short. Around 70 years if you're lucky, maybe more, maybe less. Are you chasing greatness in the areas that are most important to you? Do you know what your priorities are? Could others tell what they are if they looked at your life? If the second date on your headstone was tomorrow, how would you evaluate your life? How would others?

These are sobering questions, but they are meant to encourage. Pretending you have forever might feel better, but if it isn't the reality, then it won't actually do you any good. I've seen too many lives, too many dashes, that go out with a whimper. I've seen too many people die before their time, and leave so much of what they hoped to accomplish unfinished, not because they didn't have time, but because they didn't make the most of the time they were given. They didn't live their dash.

The great news is this: your grand slam journey has already started. You're already living your dash. Just by holding this book in your hands, you've chosen to get into the batter's box and see some pitches. You already know you don't have forever to hit the grand slam, and you're acting like it. So keep on, sister! Stick with it, brother! Chase greatness like there's no tomorrow, because someday, there won't be.

Base Study: Third Base

BRANDIE WILLIAMS (51) | *GRANITE BAY, CA*

My sister Janine was an incredible woman. She was my friend and mentor and coach in business, and so I talked to her pretty much every day about various things that were happening with my job and life. She had no children of her own, but she was the favorite aunt of all the kids.

My sister had stage four cancer and decided to fight her battle differently, rather than spending time in the hospital and going back and forth. This meant she'd made the decision to pass. With the type of cancer she had, there were few options for treatment. So she had a very honest conversation with her doctor in which she was told that she essentially had three months to live. After pursuing all the options available, she decided that it was time to go into hospice, which she said was the scariest decision she ever made, but also the most relieving decision she ever made.

Shortly after she decided to forgo further treatment, Mark invited her to share her story on a call with our company as a part of a larger discussion about "the Dash." Janine was adamant that she wanted to share with others to give them hope and encouragement because she wasn't scared anymore. She was at peace with her decision. She just knew that it was her time and took comfort from her belief in a spiritual afterlife and in heaven. Here is a short but moving excerpt from that conversation that has stuck with me:

"You know, we can always think about the future, but the future is not predicted. It's what you do in the present. It's how you listen to people in the present and enjoy those moments, those little moments of you just sitting there talking to your friend or you sitting there and having coffee with your partner or sitting in the backyard with your kids, playing baseball or listening to them play the violin. Those are the moments that you need to cherish right then and there, because you can't always plan for your future and your retirement and things like that. But I think sometimes, now that I look back, that I spent too much time worrying about what the next job might be, or wondering whether I was doing a good enough job because I might not have gotten the praise that I needed, or being so down because a meeting didn't go right that day. Those were times when I forgot to live in the present and go, 'You know what? I had a really good phone call with my best friend today,' or 'My nephew texted me today just to say hi and that he loves me.' Those are the moments you need to live in the present and appreciate because no one can guarantee the future. Even for me as I go through this, I can't predict what's coming next. I know I'm at the end. I know I'm at the end of my dash moment. I'm coming to peace with everything and realizing I did live a good life, that I don't regret many things. And, knowing that, I can see that there's hope. My family is going to be okay moving forward without me. You know, I'll probably come back as a hummingbird."

It relates back to the dash, and to not sweat the small stuff and spend time with family and friends with intention and make sure you go after those adventures in life. If you're trying to make that decision —do I jump on a plane or do I go to my son's football game?—you should go to the football game and figure out how to take the meeting later, because those are moments and flashes and memories in life that you just don't get to do over. They're once-in-a-lifetime events as we grow older.

Janine passed away almost exactly two weeks after the call. She died peacefully at home with my stepmom and her sisters around her. And right up until her last breath, she was herself. Since she's passed, I've had some of the most remarkable experiences where unless you have some kind of faith, you might not even believe. For example, when I was traveling to see my daughter who just moved to San Diego after she graduated college, I was at a store in the airport because my flight was delayed. Janine and I always used to buy matching rings; we just loved jewelry. So I was up at the register looking at the rings and the lady behind the counter looked behind me rather startled and said, "Oh my gosh, where did you come from?" I looked up and there, inside the airport, was the most beautiful monarch butterfly I've ever seen, just kind of hovering in the corner of the store in the middle of October.

Of course, my eyes filled with tears. There was a lady standing nearby and she said, "Are you okay?" I said, "I'm fine. I don't know what you believe or not, but that's my sister; her spirit is here. She brought that butterfly to this airport." The butterfly came over and landed right next to where I'd laid my wallet, and it was fluttering its wings and dancing around. And then it flew up again and just hovered there. As I told the story, everyone around me who heard it was in tears.

Death can obviously be a scary thing—it's an unknown, and we don't like unknowns. We don't know when our time will come. I think a lot of times, we take days for granted. I know I did. We think we'll always be around, and we often don't realize that our time is limited until it's too late. That's where the significance of the dash comes in, the span between the day we're born and the day we pass, so we can make sure that we're really living life to the fullest.

— Brandie Williams, *Grand Slam: Optimize your Dash*

Chapter 5
Home Plate

I can never think about the final 90 feet of the basepath without the words of the great American poet and lead singer and guitarist of Creedence Clearwater Revival, John Fogerty, coming immediately and melodically to mind:

> "Well, beat the drum and hold the
> phone
> The sun came out today
> We're born again, there's new grass on
> the field A-roundin' third, and headed
> for home
> It's a brown-eyed handsome man
> Anyone can understand the way I
> feel"[1]

Fogerty's classic song "Centerfield" captures the anticipation and excitement of baseball shared by any fan of the game, and the first verse in particular depicts that thrilling moment of "roundin' third." "Anyone can understand the way I feel," sings Fogerty.

Even for those unfamiliar with baseball, the sense of excitement and accomplishment represented by crossing home plate and completing one's trip around the bases is universally recognizable, as Fogerty suggests. All of us long for the moment in our lives where we can cross our own home plate, where we can rest, reflect, and relish our accomplishments. And all of us know the pride, no matter how big or small, of achieving something that we have worked for, even if it goes unrecognized by others.

Home plate in baseball is such a perfect image for this. It is, as one sportswriter has put it, "an open corner of the universe," a place of unlimited possibility and a place of definite accomplishment. The game of baseball starts and ends with home plate. It is the focus of every play, the place any ball to be put into play must cross, the point where every player, coach, fan, and umpire fixes their concentration for the vast majority of every game. Its width determines which pitches can be called strikes, and balls put into play must fall within lines extending out from it as their origin, which is why the plate is shaped like a pentagon instead of a square like the rest of the bases. In a way, the entire architecture and design of a baseball park takes its cues from the shape, size, and location of home plate. It is the clearly defined goal of the game of baseball, the place where everyone starts, and where everyone hopes to end up. In fact, if no one ever crosses home plate, a game of baseball could theoretically go on for eternity. (Whether that sounds more like heaven or hell might tell you something about your feelings for the sport.)

What I'm getting at here is that home plate is significant. And if you've ever watched a game of baseball, you know that every time someone crosses home plate, it is a cause for celebration.

This is because crossing home plate is actually a relatively rare occurrence in a typical baseball game. For the best teams, it happens on average around 5 times per game. For the worst teams, that average is three times per game. There were 351 shutouts in the MLB in 2022[2], which means 351 games in which a team kept its opponent from crossing home plate a *single time*. As in baseball, so in life: coming home shouldn't be taken for granted.

As we consider home plate in the grand slam life, we are reminded that not everyone crosses home plate. And far, far, fewer cross home plate after hitting a grand slam. A grand slam is a monumental achievement. Greatness is something to be *celebrated*.

So I think about home plate as a big celebration.

If you've made it to home plate, it means that you've really hit that grand slam. You've chased greatness, and on some level, you've finally caught it. You've been striving, you've been grinding, and you've been giving everything you have to achieve it. You've been intentional, you've worked with and for others, and you've lived your dash, or at least this portion of it. Home plate is the place where you can look back on your accomplishments and celebrate what you've done. It's a time to bask in your triumphs, to enjoy the fruits of your effort. It's a full-circle kind of moment where you can say, "Okay, I've achieved these things; it's time to pause, it's time to converge with the team from the dugout and celebrate together at home plate."

And if you've ever witnessed a grand slam, or any kind of walk-off hit in a baseball game, you've seen a beautiful picture of what this celebration can look like. When a walk-off home run is hit, and all the more for a grand slam, the celebration starts as soon as the ball goes over the wall in the outfield. The entire team and coaching staff rush out of the dugout and spill onto the field surrounding home plate, typically jumping around like maniacs. The trot around the bases is choreographed madness; with each step the home run hero gets closer to the pandemonium waiting at home plate. When he finally arrives at home, he is mobbed by his teammates, disappearing into a crowd of grown men, all wearing the same outfit, screaming like teenage girls at a 2001

Backstreet Boys concert. It's a sight to behold.

There are few better images of celebration in all of life, let alone in sports.

It's what the grand slam life is all about, really: achieving something truly great alongside the people that you care about the most, and celebrating that achievement with them. Home plate is the big party at the end of the grand slam. It's the reception after the wedding. It's looking back on the work of your life, on all the ground you've covered in your relentless chase for greatness, and being proud of how far you've come. Home plate is the ultimate sense of accomplishment.

The Grand Slam Cycle

The "completion" aspect of home plate is so important to the grand slam life. There must be points in your life where you feel you can genuinely rest, where you can look out on the life you've lived and feel a sense of joy in accomplishment. Endless striving is unsustainable, and we need home plates in our lives to cross, points where we have permission to rest and celebrate. I hope that comes through loud and clear here.

But just because home plate means you've completed a grand slam, it doesn't mean it has to be your finish line. One other beautiful thing about the grand slam imagery for a life of greatness is that *it's possible to hit more than one grand slam.* While it's true that every at-bat can't be a grand slam, and that grand slams will be few and far between even in a well-lived life, it's also true that grand slams don't have to be singular events. Many careers contain multiple grand slams, and so do many lives.

So home plate is certainly a moment to stop and celebrate, a time to rest and recoup. But it is also an opportunity to start thinking about that next at-bat, and to start planning for that next grand slam. There are more pitches to hit on the horizon, and more at-bats coming your way. And while you don't know how many more times you'll be in that batter's box—none of us do—you do have what's right in front of you, and you have the chance to make the most of it. There is still some length left in your dash if you're reading this book!

This is the cycle of the grand slam life. Home plate is where the game starts and ends...and where it starts again. So if you have the privilege of crossing home plate in your life, of hitting that coveted grand slam, you need to enjoy it. Find time to celebrate and relish it with others, those who helped you hit it, and those for whom you hit it. At the same time, know that just as home plate is an end, it is also a new beginning, the place where your next grand slam journey starts. So enjoy that dance party at home plate and the champagne shower in the locker room. Go wild at the ticker tape parade. Mount the home run ball in your office. And then step back into the batter's box, size up the pitcher, and swing for the fences. You've got another grand slam to hit.

Chapter 6
On Deck

Where do we go from here? We've covered our bases, we've talked about greatness, about intentionality, about focusing on others, and about living your dash. We've talked about the thrill of the chase for greatness, and about developing a burning desire to be truly great. We've *talked* about a lot of really exciting stuff. But now, it's time to put your money where your mouth is. We've *talked* plenty, it's time to go out and *do* it.

That's why the best image for the end of this book isn't home plate, it's the on-deck circle. I've told you what it takes to get to home plate, you know what greatness looks like, and you may even have a little bit of understanding of what it feels like. Now I'm tossing you the bat. You're on deck, then it's time to step into the batter's box and do your thing.

There are no guarantees for the grand slam journey that lies before you. It will be difficult. It will take effort. It will require you to make sacrifices and harness discipline that might not even seem possible to you right now. You might be facing down a pitcher with the best stuff in the league, someone who throws a triple-digit fastball and an untouchable curve. Maybe for you that's an addiction, maybe it's an uphill climb in your job that seems insurmountable, maybe you're managing a staff at a company in complete disarray, maybe it's a marriage that's on the rocks or a parent-child relationship that needs some serious attention. Whatever it is that you're facing, whatever pitches are coming your way, you've got what it takes to get around the bases. You know that to hit that grand slam you're going to need intentionality —steadfast commitment and determination to reach your goal. You're going to need others— people that can support you, and a team that motivates you to succeed. And you're going to need to remember the dash—you don't have forever, the time to start is now!

If you can keep all of these things in sight, and keep your locker open so that you are vulnerable with and accountable to others, then you're doing everything you can to put yourself in a position to succeed. All you've got to do is watch the ball come off the bat.

You can think of me as your coach. I'm standing on the third base line, cheering you on. When you look down the line while you wait for the next pitch, you're going to see me giving you the same sign over and over— swing the bat! Don't go down looking! Take a cut at the next pitch and see what happens. If you've got two strikes against you and that third pitch is coming, don't look, *swing*. I'm telling you here and now: going down looking is not an option. Swing, and keep swinging. You can't hit a grand slam if you don't swing.

Finally, I want you to hear me say this loud and clear: You can do this. I believe you're capable. If you've read this book and made it this far, you have what it takes to chase greatness. You have what it takes to hit your grand slam in life. And I'm rooting for you. I want you to go out and live your dash, to chase greatness, and to achieve your goals in life. What you've read here will give you a solid base from which to work.

So grab your bat, and step into the on-deck circle. The bases are loaded, the crowd is roaring, and the game is on the line. Your grand slam life is there for the taking.

You're up!

Notes

1. The Batter's Box

1. "Grand Slam." Wikipedia. Wikimedia Foundation, December 11, 2022. https://en.wikipedia.org/wiki/Grand_Slam.
2. "Original Grand Slam ®." Denny's. Accessed February 9, 2023. https://dennys.id/menu/original-grand-slam/.

5. Home Plate

1. Fogerty, John. "Centerfield", track 1 on Centerfield, Warner Bros., 1985, compact disc.
2. "MLB Team Shutouts." MLB Stats - MLB Team Shutouts | TeamRankings.com, December 31, 2022. https://www.teamrankings.com/mlb/stat/shutouts?date=2022-12-31.

About the Author

Photo Credit: Kia Bondurant

Mark is an Inspirational Speaker, Entrepreneur, Real Estate Investor, and Author whose burning desire is to inspire businesses, schools, nonprofits and sports teams to chase their individual and collective greatness. He combines encouragement and challenge as he walks people through the bases of Intentionality, Focusing on Others, Sense of Urgency, and the Chase. If you want to learn more about bringing Mark to speak to your group, please visit his website at www.GrandSlamBook.com by scanning the QR code below. You can also email him at

HitYourGrandSlam@gmail.com

in linkedin.com/in/mark-a-martinez-68b6187

Made in the USA
Monee, IL
23 December 2023

50426389R00079